THIS IS AMERICA'S DAY

www.castlepointbooks.com

The Castle Point Books trademark is owned by Castle Point Publishing, LLC. Castle Point books are published and distributed by St. Martin's Publishing Group.

ISBN 978-1-250-27945-3 (hardcover)
ISBN 978-1-250-27946-0 (ebook)

Our books may be purchased in bulk for promotional, educational, or business use. Please contact your local bookseller or the Macmillan Corporate and Premium Sales Department at 1-800-221-7945, extension 5442, or by email at MacmillanSpecialMarkets@macmillan.com.

First Edition: 2021

10 9 8 7 6 5 4 3 2 1

Front cover photographs (Top row, from left): Win McNamee / POOL / AFP, Tasos Katopodis/Getty Images, Patrick Semansky / POOL / AFP via Getty Images, Jonathan Ernst-Pool/Getty Images, Alex Wong/Getty Images, mccv / Shutterstock.com; (bottom row, from left): mccv / Shutterstock.com, mccv / Shutterstock.com, Andrew Harnik - Pool/Getty Images, mccv / Shutterstock.com, Patrick T. Fallon / AFP, mccv / Shutterstock.com; Back cover photographs (from left): Nicole Glass Photography / Shutterstock.com, Andrew Harnik / POOL / AFP, Kent Nishimura / Los Angeles Times via Getty Images, David Tulis - Pool/ Getty Images, lunamarina /Shutterstock.com, Shutterstock.com; Back flap photo: Patrick Semansky / POOL / AFP via Getty Images; Page 2: Patrick Semansky / POOL / AFP via Getty Images; Page 5: Nicole Glass Photography / Shutterstock.com; Page 10: Rob Carr/Getty Images; Page 18: Jane Tyska/Digital First Media/East Bay Times via Getty Images; Page 21, 85: Chip Somodevilla/Getty Images; Page 25, 89, 98: photograph by mccv / Shutterstock.com; Page 29: Julian Leshay / Shutterstock.com; Page 30: Kent Nishimura / Los Angeles Times via Getty Images; Page 33: Joshua Roberts/POOL/AFP via Getty Images; Page 34: NumenaStudios / Shutterstock.com; Page 37, 58: Jim Watson/AFP via Getty Images; Page 42: Tverdokhlib / Shutterstock.com; Page 45: Jeff Hutchens/Getty Images; Page 46: flysnowfly / Shutterstock.com; Page 53: Maverick Pictures / Shutterstock.com; Page 54: Tom Wurl / Shutterstock.com; Page 56: Al Teich / Shutterstock.com; Page 62: Tasos Katopodis/Getty Images; Page 65: Bettmann/Contributor/Getty Images; Page 66: Andrew Harnik / POOL / AFP; Page 69: Joe Guetzloff / Shutterstock.com; Page 70: lev radin / Shutterstock.com; Page 73: Nuno21 / Shutterstock.com; Page 74: David Tulis - Pool/Getty Images; Page 78: Stephanie Kenner / Shutterstock.com; Page 94: Kent Nishimura / Los Angeles Times via Getty Images; Page 97: Glynnis Jones / Shutterstock.com; Page 102: Allison C Bailey / Shutterstock.com; Page 105: Christos S / Shutterstock.com; Page 106, 122: Evan Vucci / AP/ Shutterstock; Page 110: Johnny Silvercloud / Shutterstock.com; Page 113: Ron Sachs/CNP/Getty Images; Page 114: Alex Wong/Getty Images; Page 117: Olivier Douliery / AFP; Page 121: Joshua Roberts/Reuters/Bloomberg via Getty Images; Page 124: Patrick T. Fallon / AFP; Remaining images provided under license from Shutterstock.com

THIS IS AMERICA'S DAY

INAUGURAL ADDRESS BY

PRESIDENT JOSEPH R. BIDEN, JR.

JANUARY 20, 2021

CASTLE POINT BOOKS

NEW YORK

ON JANUARY 20ᵀᴴ, 2021, AMERICA'S NEWLY ELECTED 46ᵀᴴ PRESIDENT, JOSEPH R. BIDEN, JR., DELIVERED ONE OF THE MOST STIRRING INAUGURATION SPEECHES OF ALL TIME;

a message of hope and healing when the country needed it most. *This*, he began, *is America's day*. As he continued, his words helped bolster a nation weary from cynicism and partisanship, civil unrest, racial division and injustice, and death and loss in the wake of a pandemic. From their living rooms, their classrooms, and their offices, Americans listened, transfixed, moved by something they hadn't felt in a long time: a bright awakening, a sense of possibility.

On this same day, Americans watched Kamala Harris command the stage and become the nation's first female, first African-American, first Asian-American vice-president. Doors were being opened. History was being made. Amanda Gorman reminded us, with her gift for poetry, that a new generation of pioneers was ready to climb the hills before them.

This Is America's Day is a patriotic keepsake that captures a crucial turning point for the United States and celebrates a president who is ready to "answer the call of history;" whose "whole soul is in it." With striking photography and the complete words of Joe Biden's inaugural address, this tribute captures the heart of the American story and the day Joe Biden reinvigorated his people, reminding them of their humanity, assuring them of the strength of their democracy, and offering them, at last, a common goal of unity.

THIS IS AMERICA'S DAY.

This is democracy's day.

A day of history and hope.

Of renewal and resolve.

Through a crucible for the ages
America has been tested anew and
America has risen to the challenge.

Today, we celebrate the triumph
not of a candidate, but of a cause,

THE CAUSE OF DEMOCRACY.

The will of the people
has been heard and the will
of the people has been heeded.

We have learned again that
democracy is precious.

Democracy is fragile.

And at this hour, my friends,

DEMOCRACY HAS PREVAILED.

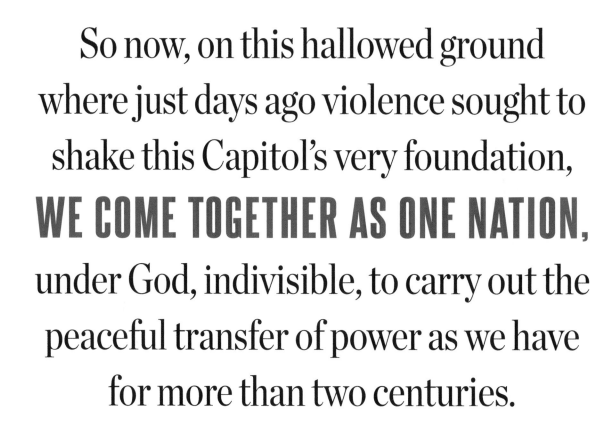

So now, on this hallowed ground where just days ago violence sought to shake this Capitol's very foundation, **WE COME TOGETHER AS ONE NATION,** under God, indivisible, to carry out the peaceful transfer of power as we have for more than two centuries.

We look ahead in our
uniquely American way—
restless, bold, optimistic—
and set our sights on
THE NATION WE KNOW WE CAN BE
and we must be.

I thank my predecessors of both
parties for their presence here.

I thank them from
the bottom of my heart.

You know the

RESILIENCE OF OUR CONSTITUTION

and the strength of our nation.

As does President Carter, who I spoke to last night but who cannot be with us today, but whom we salute for his lifetime of service.

I have just taken the sacred oath each of these patriots took—an oath first sworn by George Washington.

We the People
insure domestic Tranquility, provide for the com
and our Posterity, do ordain and establish this
ARTICLES
SOLVED

But the American story depends
not on any one of us, not on
some of us, but on all of us.

On "We the People" who seek
a more perfect Union.

THIS IS A GREAT NATION

and we are a good people.

Over the centuries through storm
and strife, in peace and in war,

WE HAVE COME SO FAR.

But we still have far to go.

We will press forward with speed and
urgency, for we have much to do in
this winter of peril and possibility.

Much to repair.

Much to restore.

Much to heal.

MUCH TO BUILD.

And much to gain.

Few periods in our nation's history have been more challenging or difficult than the one we're in now.

A ONCE-IN-A-CENTURY VIRUS

silently stalks the country.

It's taken as many lives in one year as America lost in all of World War II.

MILLIONS OF JOBS HAVE BEEN LOST.

Hundreds of thousands
of businesses closed.

A cry for racial justice some
400 years in the making moves us.

THE DREAM OF JUSTICE FOR ALL

will be deferred no longer.

A CRY FOR SURVIVAL

comes from the planet itself.
A cry that can't be any more
desperate or any more clear.

And now, a rise in political extremism, white supremacy, domestic terrorism that we must confront and we will defeat.

To overcome these challenges— to restore the soul and to **SECURE THE FUTURE OF AMERICA—** requires more than words.

It requires that
most elusive of things
in a democracy:

Unity.

UNITY.

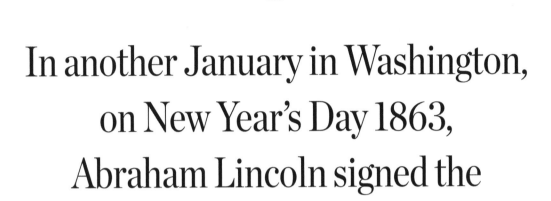

In another January in Washington,
on New Year's Day 1863,
Abraham Lincoln signed the
Emancipation Proclamation.

When he put pen to paper,
the President said,
"If my name ever goes down into
history it will be for this act and
my whole soul is in it."

MY WHOLE SOUL IS IN IT.

Today, on this January day,
my whole soul is in this:

BRINGING AMERICA TOGETHER.

Uniting our people.

And uniting our nation.

I ask every American to
join me in this cause.

UNITING TO FIGHT

the common foes we face:

Anger, resentment, hatred.

Extremism, lawlessness, violence.

Disease, joblessness, hopelessness.

WITH UNITY WE CAN DO GREAT THINGS.

Important things.

We can right wrongs.

We can put people to work in good jobs.

WE CAN TEACH OUR CHILDREN

in safe schools.

We can overcome this deadly virus.

We can reward work, rebuild
the middle class, and make
health care secure for all.

WE CAN DELIVER RACIAL JUSTICE.

We can make America,
once again, the leading force
for good in the world.

I know speaking of unity can sound to some like a foolish fantasy.

I KNOW THE FORCES THAT DIVIDE US are deep and they are real.

But I also know they are not new.

Our history has been a
constant struggle between the
American ideal that we are
all created equal and the
harsh, ugly reality that racism,
nativism, fear, and demonization
have long torn us apart.

THE BATTLE IS PERENNIAL.

Victory is never assured.

Through the Civil War,
the Great Depression, World War,
9/11, through struggle, sacrifice,
and setbacks, our "better angels"
have always prevailed.

In each of these moments,

ENOUGH OF US CAME TOGETHER

to carry all of us forward.

And, we can do so now.

History, faith, and
reason show the way,

THE WAY OF UNITY.

We can see each other not as
adversaries but as neighbors.

We can treat each other
with dignity and respect.

We can join forces,
stop the shouting, and
lower the temperature.

For without unity, there is no peace,
only bitterness and fury.

No progress,
only exhausting outrage.

No nation,
only a state of chaos.

THIS IS OUR HISTORIC MOMENT
of crisis and challenge, and
unity is the path forward.

And, we must meet this moment as
the United States of America.

If we do that, I guarantee you,
WE WILL NOT FAIL.

We have never, ever, ever failed in
America when we have acted together.

And so today,
at this time and in this place,

LET US START AFRESH.

All of us.

Let us listen to one another.

Hear one another.
See one another.

Show respect to one another.

POLITICS NEED NOT BE A RAGING FIRE

destroying everything in its path.

Every disagreement doesn't have
to be a cause for total war.

And, we must reject a culture in which
facts themselves are manipulated
and even manufactured.

My fellow Americans,
we have to be different than this.

America has to be better than this.

And, I believe

AMERICA IS BETTER THAN THIS.

Just look around.

Here we stand, in the shadow of a Capitol dome that was completed amid the Civil War, when the Union itself hung in the balance.

Yet we endured and **WE PREVAILED.**

Here we stand
looking out to the great Mall where
Dr. King spoke of his dream.

HERE WE STAND,

where 108 years ago at another
inaugural, thousands of protestors
tried to block brave women from
marching for the right to vote.

Today, we mark the swearing-in of the
first woman in American history
elected to national office —
Vice President Kamala Harris.

DON'T TELL ME THINGS CAN'T CHANGE.

Here we stand
across the Potomac from
Arlington National Cemetery,
where heroes who gave the

LAST FULL MEASURE OF DEVOTION

rest in eternal peace.

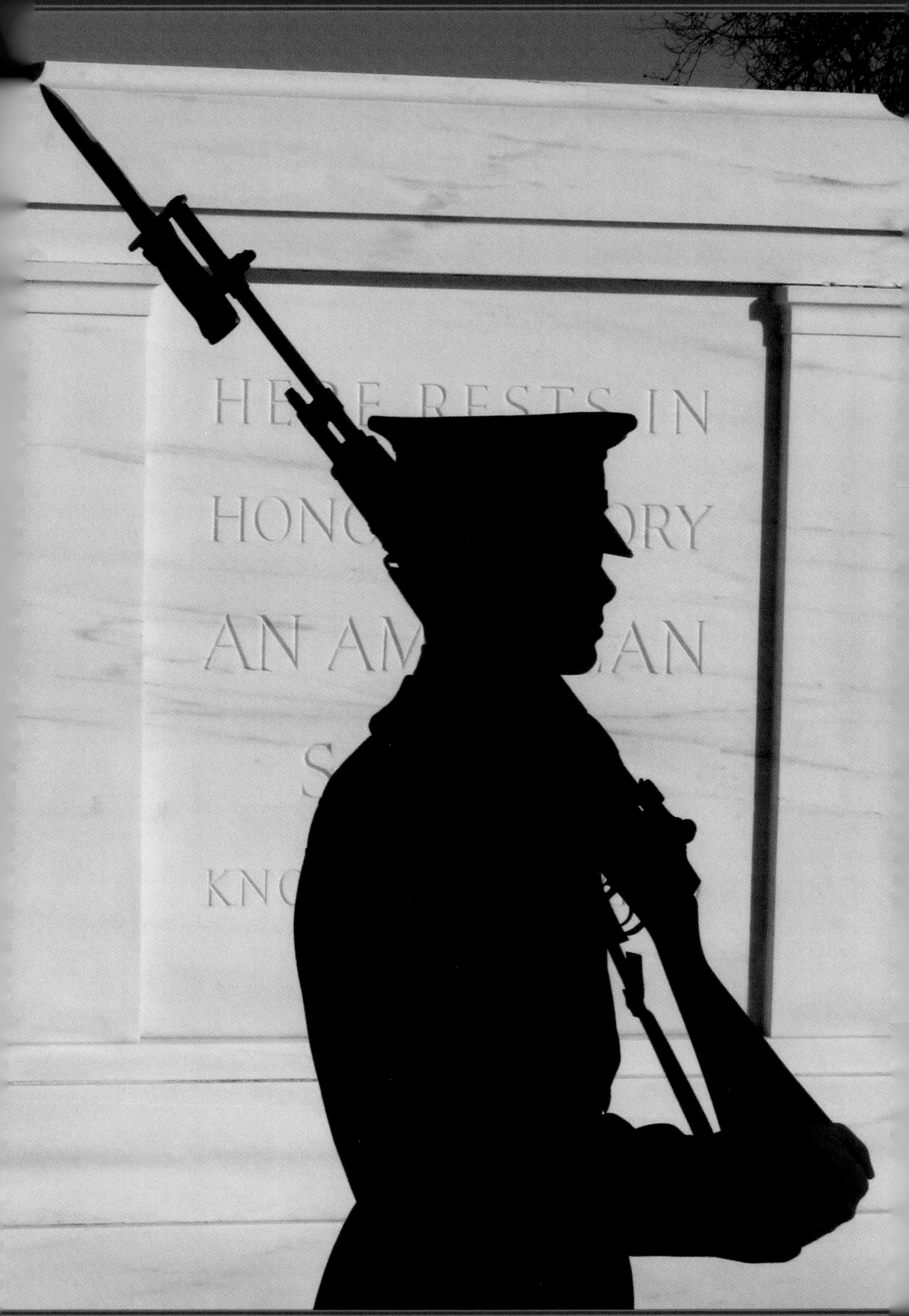

And here we stand, just days after a riotous mob thought they could use violence to silence the will of the people, to stop the work of our democracy, and to drive us from this sacred ground.

That did not happen.

IT WILL NEVER HAPPEN.

Not today.

Not tomorrow.

Not ever.

To all those who supported our campaign I am humbled by the faith you have placed in us.

To all those who did not support us, let me say this: Hear me out as we move forward.

TAKE A MEASURE OF ME AND MY HEART.

And if you still disagree, so be it.

That's democracy. That's America. The right to dissent peaceably, within the guardrails of our Republic, is perhaps our nation's greatest strength.

Yet hear me clearly:
Disagreement must not
lead to disunion.

And I pledge this to you: I will be

A PRESIDENT FOR ALL AMERICANS.

I will fight as hard for
those who did not support me
as for those who did.

Many centuries ago, Saint Augustine, a saint of my church, wrote that a people was a multitude defined by the common objects of their love.

What are the common objects we love that define us as Americans?

I think I know.

Opportunity. Security. Liberty.

DIGNITY. RESPECT. HONOR.

And, yes, the truth.

Recent weeks and months have
taught us a painful lesson.

There is truth and there are lies.

Lies told for power and for profit.

And each of us has

A DUTY AND RESPONSIBILITY,

as citizens, as Americans, and
especially as leaders—leaders who
have pledged to honor our Constitution
and protect our nation—to defend
the truth and to defeat the lies.

I understand that many Americans view the future with some fear and trepidation.

I understand they worry about their jobs, about taking care of their families, about

WHAT COMES NEXT.

I get it.

But the answer is not to turn inward, to retreat into competing factions, distrusting those who don't look like you do, or worship the way you do, or don't get their news from the same sources you do.

WE MUST END THIS UNCIVIL WAR

that pits red against blue, rural versus urban, conservative versus liberal.

We can do this if we open our souls instead of hardening our hearts.

If we show a little tolerance and humility.

If we're willing to stand in the other person's shoes just for a moment. Because here is the thing about life: There is no accounting for what fate will deal you.

THERE ARE SOME DAYS WHEN WE NEED A HAND.

There are other days when we're called on to lend one.

That is how we must be with one another.

And, if we are this way, our country will be stronger, more prosperous, more ready for the future.

My fellow Americans, in the work ahead of us, we will need each other.

We will need all our strength **TO PERSEVERE THROUGH THIS DARK WINTER.**

We are entering what may well be the toughest and deadliest period of the virus.

We must set aside the politics and finally face this pandemic as one nation.

I promise you this: as the Bible says, weeping may endure for a night but

JOY COMETH IN THE MORNING.

We will get through this, together.

The world is watching today.

So here is my message
to those beyond our borders:
America has been tested and we
have come out stronger for it.

WE WILL REPAIR OUR ALLIANCES

and engage with the world once again.

Not to meet yesterday's challenges,
but today's and tomorrow's.

We will lead not merely by the example of our power but by

THE POWER OF OUR EXAMPLE.

We will be a strong and trusted partner for peace, progress, and security.

We have been through so
much in this nation.

And, in my first act as President,
I would like to ask you to join me
in a moment of silent prayer to

REMEMBER ALL THOSE WE LOST

this past year to the pandemic.

To those 400,000 fellow Americans—
mothers and fathers, husbands and
wives, sons and daughters, friends,
neighbors, and co-workers.

WE WILL HONOR THEM

by becoming the people and nation we know we can and should be.

Let us say a silent prayer for those who lost their lives, for those they left behind, and for our country.

Amen.

THIS IS A TIME OF TESTING.

We face an attack on
democracy and on truth.

A raging virus.

Growing inequity.

The sting of systemic racism.

A climate in crisis.

America's role in the world.

Any one of these would be enough
to challenge us in profound ways.

But the fact is we face them all at once, presenting this nation with the gravest of responsibilities.

NOW WE MUST STEP UP.

All of us.

IT IS A TIME FOR BOLDNESS,

for there is so much to do.

And this is certain.

We will be judged, you and I,
for how we resolve the
cascading crises of our era.

Will we rise to the occasion?

Will we master this rare
and difficult hour?

Will we meet our obligations
and pass along a new and better
world for our children?

I believe we must and

I BELIEVE WE WILL.

And when we do, we will write the
next chapter in the American story.

It's a story that might sound something
like a song that means a lot to me.

It's called "American Anthem" and there
is one verse that stands out for me:

"The work and prayers

of centuries have brought us to this day

WHAT SHALL BE OUR LEGACY?

What will our children say?...

Let me know in my heart

When my days are through

America

America

I GAVE MY BEST TO YOU."

Let us add our own work and prayers to the unfolding story of our nation.

If we do this, then when our days are through, our children and our children's children will say of us, they gave their best.

They did their duty.

THEY HEALED A BROKEN LAND.

My fellow Americans, I close today
where I began, with a sacred oath.

Before God and all of you I give you my word.

I will always level with you.

I will defend the Constitution.

I will defend our democracy.

I will defend America.

I WILL GIVE MY ALL IN YOUR SERVICE

thinking not of power, but of possibilities.

Not of personal interest, but of the public good.

And together, we shall write

AN AMERICAN STORY OF HOPE, NOT FEAR.

Of unity, not division.

Of light, not darkness.

An American story of
decency and dignity.

Of love and of healing.

Of greatness and of goodness.

May this be the story that guides us.

THE STORY THAT INSPIRES US.

The story that tells ages yet to come that we answered the call of history.

We met the moment.

That democracy and hope,
truth and justice, did not die
on our watch but thrived.

That our America

SECURED LIBERTY AT HOME

and stood once again as a
beacon to the world.

That is what we owe our forebearers, one another, and generations to follow.

So, with purpose and resolve

WE TURN TO THE TASKS OF OUR TIME.

Sustained by faith.

Driven by conviction.

And, devoted to one another
and to this country we love
with all our hearts.

MAY GOD BLESS AMERICA

and may God protect our troops.

Thank you, America.